ABERDEEN
CITY CENTRE
HISTORY TOUR

ACKNOWLEDGEMENTS

This publication has been researched and collated by staff of Aberdeen City Libraries, with grateful thanks to a library volunteer who assisted with the project.

First published 2017

Amberley Publishing
The Hill, Stroud,
Gloucestershire, GL5 4EP
www.amberley-books.com

Copyright © Aberdeen City Council, 2017
Map contains Ordnance Survey data © Crown copyright and database right [2017]

The right of Aberdeen City Council to be identified as the Author of this work has been asserted in accordance with the Copyrights, Designs and Patents Act 1988.

ISBN 978 1 4456 6658 7 (print)
ISBN 978 1 4456 6659 4 (ebook)

British Library Cataloguing in Publication Data.
A catalogue record for this book is available from the British Library.

Origination by Amberley Publishing.
Printed in Great Britain.

INTRODUCTION

Aberdeen is a vibrant city situated between the rivers Dee and Don with a rich cultural and architectural heritage. The city is currently undergoing a visual transformation with new developments such as Marischal Square and the Art Gallery extension dominating the skyline.

With the increased interest in family and local history and as Scotland celebrates the Year of History, Heritage and Archaeology in 2017, it is appropriate to reflect on Aberdeen's heritage. This new publication gives the reader a glimpse of the past during a tour around the historical city centre and the distinctive conservation area of Old Aberdeen.

Aberdeen City Centre Through Time drew upon the extensive photographic collections of Aberdeen Art Gallery & Museums, Aberdeen City & Shire Archives and the Local Studies service of the Central Library to reflect the evolving city and the changing urban landscape.

In contrast the reader can follow a route through the streets starting in Holburn Street (constructed in 1807 as the 'great south road'), and finishing back on Union Street, after a glimpse into the history of buildings, streets and areas along the way, some of which have long since disappeared. A second tour takes the reader into Old Aberdeen, with its fifteenth-century college, medieval cathedral and quaint streets.

During 2017 Aberdeen Central Library will be celebrating 125 years since it was opened by Andrew Carnegie on 5 July 1892, making this the perfect opportunity to showcase new images specifically from the library's collections, many of which can be accessed online from the Silver City Vault.

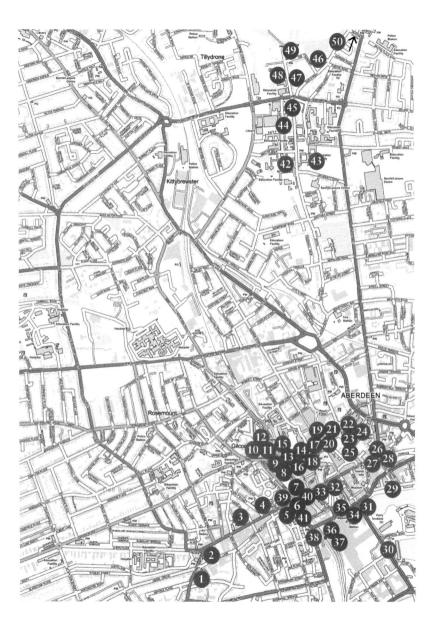

KEY

City Centre
1. Holburn Street
2. Holburn Junction
3. Corner of Union Street and Union Row
4. Corner of Union Street and Huntly Street
5. Crown Street
6. Corner of Union Street and Bridge Street
7. Union Terrace Gardens, looking South
8. Denburn Valley, looking North
9. Denburn Viaduct
10. Central Library and St Mark's Church
11. Rosemount Viaduct
12. His Majesty's Theatre
13. Schoolhill Station and Cowdray Hall
14. Aberdeen Art Gallery and Gray's School of Art on Schoolhill
15. Woolmanhill, looking South
16. Triple Kirks
17. Robert Gordon's College
18. Central School, looking East
19. Site of George Jamesone's House, Schoolhill
20. Schoolhill, looking East towards Marischal College
21. Upperkirkgate
22. Marischal College Quadrangle
23. Broad Street, East Side
24. Marischal College Entrance
25. Marischal College from St Nicholas Kirk
26. Castlegate, looking East
27. Castlegate, looking West
28. Marischal Street
29. Upper and Victoria Docks
30. Albert Basin
31. Market Street, looking North
32. The Green, looking East
33. The Green to the Back Wynd Stairs
34. Guild Street, looking West
35. The Tivoli
36. Guild Street, looking East
37. Joint Station
38. Bridge Street, looking towards Union Street from Guild Street
39. Corner of Union Terrace with Prince Albert Statue
40. Union Bridge, looking East
41. Union Bridge, looking West

Old Aberdeen
42. Powis Gates/College Bounds
43. King's College
44. High Street
45. Town House
46. Don Street
47. Bede House
48. Chanonry
49. St Machar's Cathedral
50. Brig o' Balgownie

CITY CENTRE
1. HOLBURN STREET, LOOKING TOWARDS UNION STREET JUNCTION

Our history tour starts in Holburn Street, just north of Great Western Road, looking towards Union Street in the distance. Holburn Street was constructed in 1807 as the 'great south road', connecting the recently opened Union Street to the Bridge of Dee – the entrance to the city from the south. The domed tower at the far left was added in 1891 to Holburn Parish Church, which had opened in 1836.

2. HOLBURN JUNCTION

Holburn Junction, looking west towards Alford Place (right) and
Holburn Street (left). The square tower of Christ's College (formerly
Free Church Divinity College) is seen in the distance at what was known
as Babbie Law's Corner, named after Barbara Law's grocery shop.
The junction appears quite busy with traffic and pedestrians crossing
at the Belisha Beacon with Chivas grocers on the left. A Corporation
tram is approaching Union Street alongside a No. 25 bus.

HOLBURN JUNCTION ("BABBIE LAW") ABERDEEN

3. CORNER OF UNION STREET AND UNION ROW

Designed by renowned Aberdeen architect T. Scott Sutherland, the Majestic Cinema was opened in December 1936, closing its doors in September 1973 after showing its last film, *Kelly's Heroes*. The photograph here shows the cinema very much in use in 1966, with screenings of *The Professionals* and *Jason and the Argonauts*. Following the cinema's closure, the entire block up to the corner of Union Row was taken down and replaced with modern buildings.

4. CORNER OF UNION STREET AND HUNTLY STREET

One of the earliest buildings to appear on the western section of Union Street was Crimonmogate's House, designed in the early 1800s by the architect John Smith for Patrick Milne of Crimonmogate, near Fraserburgh. It later became the home of the Royal Northern Club, but both it and the property next door, then occupied by the YMCA, were demolished. They were replaced in the 1960s by a block of shop units.

5. CROWN STREET

This view of Crown Street shows a double set of tramlines, together with the overhead electricity cables. The turreted building to the left was the General Post Office, designed by architect W. T. Oldrieve. The building in Scots Baronial style with granite detailing was opened in 1907 by Sidney Buxton, the postmaster general. It cost over £55,000. To the right centre of the photograph is another superb Edwardian edifice – the Prudential Building by Paul Waterhouse, 1910.

6. CORNER OF UNION STREET AND BRIDGE STREET

The Palace Hotel opened in 1873 when its street level was occupied by Pratt and Keith, drapers and house furnishers. This hotel was bought by the Great North of Scotland Railway, later LNER. After a catastrophic fire in October 1941, the building was demolished in the 1950s when the C&A clothes chain built their store. C&A moved into the Bon Accord Centre in the 1990s, and the building was converted into a Travelodge hotel and shops.

7. UNION TERRACE GARDENS, LOOKING SOUTH

Union Bridge and the chimney of Hadden's textile mill in the Green act as the backdrop to this view of Union Terrace Gardens. Union Bridge was opened in 1805 to bridge the Denburn Valley, which then allowed the development of the western part of Union Street. The former Belmont Congregational Church, seen on the left, opened in 1865 but has now found a new role as a nightclub.

8. DENBURN VALLEY, LOOKING NORTH

The Denburn Valley railway was constructed around 1867 and Union Terrace Gardens with its bandstand was laid out a few years later. The closeness of the railway led to the gardens being nicknamed the 'Trainie Park'. The bandstand was removed in the 1930s. A dual carriageway now runs underneath the Denburn Viaduct, built to replace the iron footbridge that provided access for residents of the Rosemount area over the Denburn and the railway.

9. DENBURN VIADUCT

The trio of buildings sometimes referred to as Education, Salvation and Damnation were not yet complete in this 1890s view along the Denburn Viaduct over the railway line. Education (Aberdeen Public Library) and Salvation (Free South Church, now St Mark's) were followed by Damnation when His Majesty's Theatre was opened in 1906 – its glass extension was added in 2005. W. Grant Stevenson's impressive bronze statue of William Wallace was erected in 1888.

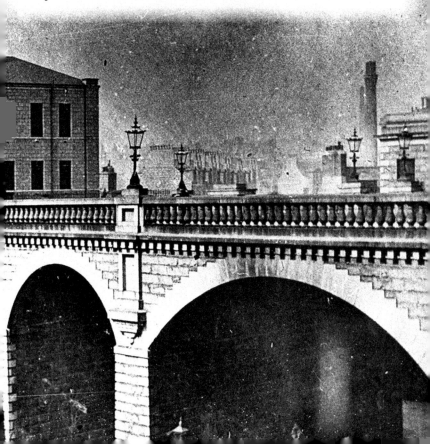

10. CENTRAL LIBRARY AND ST MARK'S CHURCH

Aberdeen Public Library was opened by Andrew Carnegie in July 1892 on Rosemount Viaduct on a site adjacent to the Free South Church (now St Mark's), which had opened for worship a few months earlier in March. The library was extended at its west end in 1905 to form what became known as the Commercial Library and Reading Room, with the Children's Library on the upper floor.

11. ROSEMOUNT VIADUCT

This photograph shows Rosemount Viaduct, which was designed in 1886 by William Boulton to connect Schoolhill with Rosemount. The Central Library and St Mark's Church can be seen on the left and in the distance are properties on the corner of Blackfriars Street. The architect James Matthews, who was Provost of Aberdeen from 1883 to 1886, is especially associated with the Rosemount-Schoolhill project. Overhead tram cables are visible but horse-drawn transport is still very evident.

12. HIS MAJESTY'S THEATRE

His Majesty's Theatre was designed by Frank Matcham and opened in 1906 with a performance of *Little Red Riding Hood*. In the foreground is the statue of Prince Albert, created by Baron Carlo Marochetti. It was relocated from the southern end of Union Terrace, where it was unveiled by Queen Victoria on a very wet day in October 1863. Her diary notes that it is 'rather small for out of doors, but fine and like'.

13. SCHOOLHILL STATION AND COWDRAY HALL

Looking across Union Terrace Gardens towards the war memorial, the Cowdray Hall and Art Gallery can be seen. Houses on Blackfriars Street were demolished to make way for the Cowdray Hall and the city's war memorial, which was unveiled in 1925. The granite lion was created by Aberdeen sculptor William McMillan.

Schoolhill railway station stood in the shadow of His Majesty's Theatre. The station was closed to passenger traffic in 1937, though this building remained as a café until the 1980s.

SCHOOLHILL STATION

14. ABERDEEN ART GALLERY AND GRAY'S SCHOOL OF ART ON SCHOOLHILL

The Art Gallery was designed by local architect Alexander Marshall Mackenzie on the site of a medieval Dominican friary – elements of their buildings, possessions and burials have been discovered during various site excavations. The Art School, founded by John Gray, was also built in 1885. Gray's School of Art became part of Robert Gordon University, and was relocated to the Garthdee area in 1965. The central gateway leads to Robert Gordon's College.

15. WOOLMANHILL, LOOKING SOUTH

This residential area of Woolmanhill, just opposite the Triple Kirks on Schoolhill, was cleared to make way for the Denburn dual carriageway. The street hidden behind the Woolmanhill houses was Blackfriars Street, and the properties at its junction with Schoolhill were demolished in the 1920s for the war memorial and Cowdray Hall. The tenements on the right were known as Black's Buildings.

16. TRIPLE KIRKS

The Triple Kirks, with its distinctive red-brick spire, was designed by Aberdeen architect Archibald Simpson for the East, South and West Free Church congregations in 1843. This view also shows houses at Mutton Brae, many of which were demolished during the construction of the Denburn Valley railway line. Sections of the church were later removed during the building of the dual carriageway, leaving the spire and remaining church buildings undeveloped.

17. ROBERT GORDON'S COLLEGE

The Auld Hoose is the oldest part of the eighteenth-century Robert Gordon's Hospital, designed for the maintenance and education of boys who were the sons of 'poor and indigent' burgesses of Aberdeen. Robert Gordon was an Aberdeen merchant who made his fortune trading in Eastern Europe. Now known as Robert Gordon's College, this co-educational private school has been much extended, but the original building by William Adam remains virtually unchanged.

18. CENTRAL SCHOOL, LOOKING EAST

The Central Higher Grade School was opened in November 1905 for pupils aged twelve to fifteen coming from the town's elementary schools, with over 1,000 on the roll initially. In 1954, it was renamed as Aberdeen Academy. When it closed in 1969, the pupils moved to the new Hazlehead Academy. This building became a resources centre for the Department of Education and then in the late 1990s it became The Academy shopping centre.

The Central School

Aberdeen

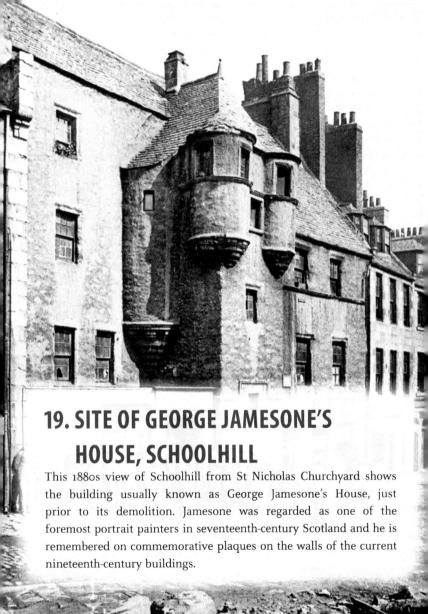

19. SITE OF GEORGE JAMESONE'S HOUSE, SCHOOLHILL

This 1880s view of Schoolhill from St Nicholas Churchyard shows the building usually known as George Jamesone's House, just prior to its demolition. Jamesone was regarded as one of the foremost portrait painters in seventeenth-century Scotland and he is remembered on commemorative plaques on the walls of the current nineteenth-century buildings.

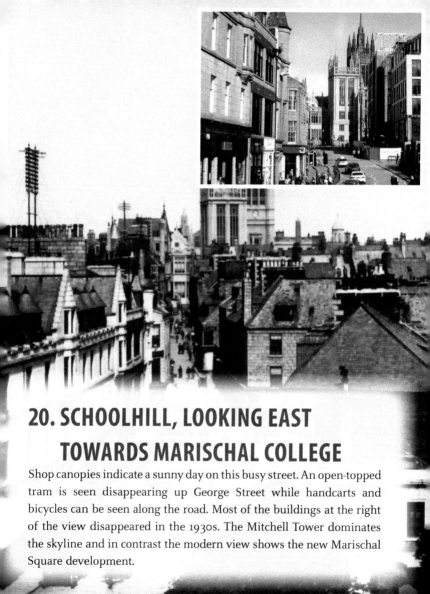

20. SCHOOLHILL, LOOKING EAST TOWARDS MARISCHAL COLLEGE

Shop canopies indicate a sunny day on this busy street. An open-topped tram is seen disappearing up George Street while handcarts and bicycles can be seen along the road. Most of the buildings at the right of the view disappeared in the 1930s. The Mitchell Tower dominates the skyline and in contrast the modern view shows the new Marischal Square development.

21. UPPERKIRKGATE

The granite splendour of Marischal College and the Mitchell Tower are the backdrop to this view of the Upperkirkgate from Schoolhill, at the junction with St Nicholas Street and George Street. The grassy area to the right was developed as the St Nicholas Shopping Centre in the 1980s, followed by the Bon Accord Centre in the 1990s.

UPPER KIRKGA
MARISCHAL COLLEG

AND
BERDEEN.

22. MARISCHAL COLLEGE QUADRANGLE

This 1880s view shows the quadrangle of Marischal College as built by Archibald Simpson in 1837–44. The obelisk, later relocated to the Duthie Park, was erected in 1860 in memory of Sir James McGrigor, graduate of Marischal College who became Director-General of the Army Medical Department. In the 1890s rebuilding works by Alexander Marshall Mackenzie included the creation of the central Mitchell Tower.

23. BROAD STREET, EAST SIDE

Dating to the late nineteenth century, this image shows the range of seventeenth- and eighteenth-century buildings lining this venerable street. The tenement on the far right was once home to the future Lord Byron and his mother when he attended the old Grammar School on Schoolhill. Today the splendid façade of Marischal College, designed by Alexander Marshall Mackenzie, completes the east side of the street in English Perpendicular architectural style.

24. MARISCHAL COLLEGE ENTRANCE

The nineteenth-century arched gateway from Broad Street to Marischal College and Greyfriars Church contained a heraldic panel showing the coat of arms of George Keith, 5th Earl Marischal. In 1593 Keith founded the college in the old Greyfriars monastery buildings. When the new frontage was created, a series of coats of arms to commemorate the history and benefactors of the university was installed above the gateway.

25. MARISCHAL COLLEGE FROM ST NICHOLAS KIRK

The sparkling Kemnay granite of the newly created frontage to the historic Marischal College contrasts with the jumble of buildings in the historic Guestrow area in the foreground, of which only the turreted Provost Skene's House now remains after slum clearances during the 1930s. Great celebrations took place when the new building was opened by Edward VII and Queen Alexandra in September 1906. Marischal College is now the headquarters of Aberdeen City Council.

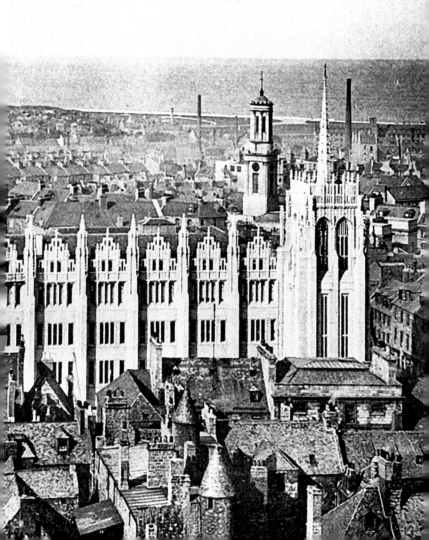

26. CASTLEGATE, LOOKING EAST

The Castlegate was Aberdeen's ancient marketplace. The Market Cross, erected in 1686 by John Montgomery, master mason, was the focal point for meetings and weekly markets while the Timmer Market, specialising in wooden goods and toys, was held annually in August. Several trams are travelling on the loop lines past the Salvation Army Citadel, which opened in June 1896. The statue of the 5th Duke of Gordon was relocated to Golden Square in 1952.

CASTLE STR

AND SALVATION ARMY CITADEL, ABERDEEN

27. CASTLEGATE, LOOKING WEST

This image is looking west along Union Street from the Castlegate, showing the Tollbooth and Town House spires. The building at the corner of Union Street and King Street was designed by Archibald Simpson as the North of Scotland Bank, later Clydesdale Bank. After refurbishment it opened in 1997 as a pub named The Archibald Simpson. In the centre was Jimmy Hay's, the popular Royal Athenaeum restaurant, originally a newsroom, which was badly damaged by fire in 1973.

28. MARISCHAL STREET

Plans for Marischal Street were drawn up in 1767 and the more direct, if steep, access from the Castlegate to the Quayside was laid out on the newly cleared site. The decorative lamps of the Royal Oak public house in 1949 have long since gone, but the eighteenth-century buildings in this historic street still remain.

29. UPPER AND VICTORIA DOCKS

This 1904 image shows steam and sail vessels along with the Royal Naval Reserve training ship HMS *Clyde* in the Upper and Victoria Docks, which were separated by the Regent swing bridge. Vessels could only access these docks at high tide, but in the 1970s they were converted to full tidal working with twenty-four-hour access by removing the dock gates, along with St Clement's and Regent bridges.

30. ALBERT BASIN

The mixture of steam and sailing vessels in this nineteenth-century view of Albert Basin reflects the prosperity of the fishing industry in Aberdeen at this period. The herring drifters in the foreground of the picture could reach to over 60 feet in length, with a mast height equal to that. They had a crew of six or seven who were often members of the same family.

31. MARKET STREET, LOOKING NORTH

Market Street, which connected Union Street to the busy harbour area, took its name from the New Market, opened in 1842 by the New Market Co. The building on the right was originally a post office before becoming the Labour Exchange. Other buildings remaining today include the Douglas Hotel, which has had its exterior façade cleaned following refurbishment. The Mechanics Institution (now the Rox Hotel) housed Aberdeen's first public lending library, which opened in 1886.

32. THE GREEN, LOOKING EAST

The curved wall of the popular New Market dominates this view of the Green, where farming folk are gathered round the eighteenth-century 'Mannie in the Green' street well to sell their butter, eggs, vegetables and flowers at the Friday Market. The New Market was controversially demolished in 1972 to be replaced by the Aberdeen Market and the 'Mannie' returned to his original home in the Castlegate.

33. THE GREEN TO THE BACK WYND STAIRS

The Green was originally on the main route through the city before the construction of Union Street on a series of arches overlooking this area. The medieval house occupied by John Buchan, baker, formerly known as Aedie's Lodging, stood at the foot of the Back Wynd stairs leading up to Union Street until it was demolished in 1914. The golden teapot sign on John Adam's tea and coffee shop (on the right-hand side of the image) disappeared when the premises closed.

34. GUILD STREET, LOOKING WEST

In the foreground is Fidler's Well, erected and dedicated in 1857 to Dr William Guild by Alexander Fidler, a coal broker in Aberdeen. Originally intended for horses, it later had two iron cups fixed to it. Fidler died in 1885 but his well remained here until 1957 when it was moved to the Duthie Park. In 2002 it was moved to its current location beside Trinity Hall on Holburn Street.

35. THE TIVOLI

Originally opened as Her Majesty's Opera House in 1872, the building was refurbished in 1909 by renowned theatre architect Frank Matcham. It reopened in 1910 under the name of the Tivoli. A popular theatre, many well-known performers appeared on its stage including W. C. Fields, Tony Hancock and Andy Stewart. Becoming a bingo hall in 1966, it finally closed its doors to the public in 1997. Following refurbishment, it is again open to theatregoers.

36. GUILD STREET, LOOKING EAST

The Criterion Bar is seen next to the Tivoli Theatre on a rather peaceful Guild Street. The bar closed in 2012 but planning permission was granted in 2013 to convert it to retail premises. The area on the right has seen massive changes as part of the Union Square development. Guild Street takes its name from Dr William Guild, principal of King's College and benefactor of Aberdeen Incorporated Trades.

37. JOINT STATION

The railway reached Aberdeen in the 1850s and a joint station to link the lines from the north and south of the city was opened in 1867. The foundation stone for this replacement main station was laid in 1913, and, unusually for Aberdeen, features a sandstone frontage. Today this area is much altered and most of the station frontage is contained within the Union Square shopping centre.

38. BRIDGE STREET, LOOKING TOWARDS UNION STREET FROM GUILD STREET

Bridge Street was built between 1865 and 1867 and arches over the old route into the city, which led from the Bridge of Dee along the Hardgate, via Windmill Brae and the Green into the heart of the city. The gap between the buildings on the left leads to the steep stairway to Crown Terrace, and on the corner of Guild Street was the booking office for the suburban railways, now renovated as commercial premises.

39. CORNER OF UNION TERRACE WITH PRINCE ALBERT STATUE

Mann's Grand Hotel (later the Caledonian), seen on the left flying the flag, was opened in 1892 by Charles Mann, the former owner of the Palace Hotel. The statue of Prince Albert was relocated to the north end of Union Terrace in 1914 to make way for the statue of Edward VII. The imposing building on the left was the Northern Assurance building, known locally as the Monkey House, now a restaurant.

40. UNION BRIDGE, LOOKING EAST

The first coach travelled over Union Bridge in 1805. The bridge was widened in the early 1900s when the iconic plaques and leopard finials popularly known as Kelly cats were installed. Shops were added on the south side in the 1960s. On the right is Trinity Hall, the home of the Seven Incorporated Trades of Aberdeen until they relocated to new premises on Holburn Street and this building became part of the Trinity shopping centre.

41. UNION BRIDGE, LOOKING WEST

In the 1880s this splendid view was to be had from Union Bridge, looking west along Union Street with the Palace Hotel on the left and the Northern Assurance building at the corner of Union Terrace. The distant spires belong to Free Churches erected in 1868–69 – Gilcomston (right) and the West Church of St Andrew (left), better known as Langstone Church.

OLD ABERDEEN
42. POWIS GATES/COLLEGE BOUNDS

This unusual gateway formed the entrance to the Powis estate, owned by the Leslie family, and was built in 1834. These oriental-style towers with minarets and the coats of arms of the Powis lairds have provoked much interest over the years. The estate was taken over by Aberdeen Town Council in the 1930s and a housing scheme was laid out, while Powis House has recently been refurbished as its community centre.

43. KING'S COLLEGE

King's College was founded by Bishop William Elphinstone in 1495 and the chapel with its crown tower was completed in 1506. After it was blown down in a storm in 1633 it was rebuilt, and the building has recently undergone extensive conservation works to its fabric. In 1860 the fusion of King's and Marischal Colleges took place to form the University of Aberdeen.

44. HIGH STREET

For centuries Old Aberdeen was a burgh in its own right, leading a completely separate existence with its own university, cathedral and town council until it merged with the city of Aberdeen in 1891. The High Street with its clay-pantiled roof forms part of the historic route north out of the city. Today it is the main thoroughfare through what is now mainly the University of Aberdeen's campus.

45. TOWN HOUSE

Old Aberdeen Town House was built in 1788 by George Jaffray, at the end
of the High Street at its junction with the Chanonry on the left and Don
Street on the right. The construction of St Machar Drive in the 1920s cut
through the buildings to the rear of the Town House. This building has
fulfilled many functions including a Masonic lodge and public library,
before reopening in 2013 as the university's King's Museum.

46. DON STREET

This peaceful view reflects Old Aberdeen's historic nature since Don Street led from the High Street to the Brig o' Balgownie over the River Don as the old route north from the city. It passes St Machar's Cathedral, through the lands of the old Seaton Estate, now Seaton Park, and university student halls of residence before reaching the picturesque Brig o' Balgownie.

47. BEDE HOUSE

The rubble-built structure of the Bede House at Nos 20–22 Don Street dates from 1676, but from 1787 it housed eight Bedesmen – poor, single men aged over sixty. The triangular fish hakes on the wall date from a period when dried salted fish was a staple part of the diet in the winter months. The house is now a private dwelling, while a sheltered housing complex named Bede House Court was opened nearby in 1964.

48. CHANONRY

The tree-lined Chanonry originally contained the homes or manses of the canons (clergy) of St Machar's Cathedral but its high granite walls with sloped coping stones now protect the 11-acre Cruickshank Botanic Garden and several eighteenth- and nineteenth-century houses set well back in spacious grounds. After the Chanonry reaches the medieval St Machar's Cathedral, it curves to the east to join Don Street.

49. ST MACHAR'S CATHEDRAL

Legend has it that St Machar chose this site because St Columba had asked him to build a church where a river bends like a bishop's staff. Today's cathedral has undergone a series of reconstructions beginning in the thirteenth century. The large central tower and belfry built by Bishop Elphinstone collapsed in 1688 but the west towers remain. In 1520 Bishop Dunbar created an oak ceiling displaying forty-eight heraldic shields representing religious and political figures.

50. BRIG O' BALGOWNIE

This picturesque fourteenth-century bridge, now restricted to pedestrian use, was the only access over the River Don to the north of Aberdeen prior to the construction of the Bridge of Don in the 1820s. Its single pointed Gothic arch spans a deep dark pool known as Black Nook. Many of the people who lived nearby were salmon fishers and in the 1950s a restoration scheme brought a number of their cottages back to life.

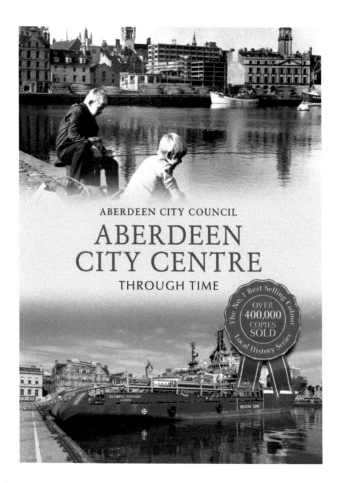